C0-DVS-737

HANDS TO HANDS

HAND CLAPPING SONGS AND GAMES FROM AROUND THE WORLD

AIMEE CURTIS PFITZNER

Layout and Editing, Brent M. Holl
Associate Editors, Karen Holl and Michael R. Nichols
Cover Design and Illustrations, Aimee Curtis Pfitzner

Printed and Distributed by Beatin' Path Publications, LLC
302 East College Street, Bridgewater, VA 22812
www.beatinpathpublications.com

© 2015 Aimee Curtis Pfitzner. All rights reserved including public performance for profit.
ISBN: 978-0-9963591-0-8

No part of this publication may be reproduced, stored in a retrieval system or transmitted in any form or by any means, electronic, mechanical, photocopying, recording or otherwise, without the prior permission of the copyright owner.

Every effort was made to authenticate these songs from folk and oral traditions; errors will be corrected in further printings.

Supplemental resources are available online at http://bppub.net/AimeeCurtisPfitzner. Included are full color visuals in .pdf and .jpg formats suitable for presentation stations or projection and videos of many games.

Purchasers can request login information to gain access to these materials at http://bppub.net/AimeeCurtisPfitzner.

CONTENTS

Pedagogy

Clapping songs and games are significant to every child's individual development. These songs and games are physically active ways to teach and reinforce many musical concepts, particularly steady beat and rhythm. The ability to keep a beat and understand a rhythm are skills that impact the remainder of the child's life. A child will use these skills to sing, play, and read. Breaking down a word into syllables is, in essence, a rhythmic skill that together with beat is an essential element in reading.

While actively engaging both the body and the brain, the motion of hand clapping benefits both children and adults. Clapping songs and games involve aural (listening), oral, physical, visual tracking, and sequencing motor skills (thinking about what movement comes next). Equally important is the social-emotional connection of collaborative work and play that hand clapping songs and games inherently provide. In our digital age, it is important for students to connect face to face and eye to eye, thus experiencing physical connections with others. Many hand clapping songs and games cross the mid-line of the body, further developing the connectivity of the right and left sides of the brain. Activation of the cerebral cortex has been studied using MRI testing where participants performed various hand movements; hand clapping movements evoked the most significant activation of this area of the brain.

Hand clapping songs and games have also been shown to improve cognitive skills. A 2010 study conducted by Dr. Idit Sulkin, of the Ben-Gurion University Music Science Lab, found that young children (particularly ages six to ten) who engage in hand-clapping games and songs have neater handwriting, better spelling and finer writing skills. As part of the study, Dr. Sulkin engaged children in several elementary school classrooms in either a music appreciation program sanctioned by the board of education or hand clapping songs for a period of ten weeks. "Within a very short period of time, the children who until then hadn't taken part in such activities caught up in their cognitive abilities to those who did," Sulkin says. However, the improved abilities were only demonstrated by the group of children participating in the hand clapping activities.

Dr. Sulkin observed, "...these activities serve as a developmental platform to enhance children's needs — emotional, sociological, physiological, and cognitive.

It's a transition stage that leads them to the next phases of growing up." Interestingly, Dr. Sulkin also found that when adults participated in hand clapping songs and games they reported feeling more focused, alert, and less stressed.

Concentration, sequencing and memory are also reasons to add clapping songs and games to activities in (and out) of the classroom. Hand clapping songs and games are an integral part of child development and a valuable resource to parents and teachers. Music teachers especially will find a rich source of material for teaching concepts and skills, not only satisfying from a pedagogical perspective, but highly engaging and fun as well.

Sources
American Associates, Ben-Gurion University of the Negev. "Hand-clapping songs improve motor and cognitive skills, research shows." ScienceDaily. ScienceDaily, 3 May 2010.

http://www.missjaimeot.com/why-you-should-teach-your-child-clapping-games/
Why You Should Teach Your Child Clapping Games, 7 November, 2014.

www.sciencedaily.com/releases/2010/04/100428090954.html. The cortical effect of clapping in the human brain: A functional MRI study.

Kim, M. J., Hong, J. H., Jang, S. H. College of Medicine, Yeungnam University, Taegu, Republic of Korea. PMID: 21447906 [PubMed - indexed for MEDLINE].

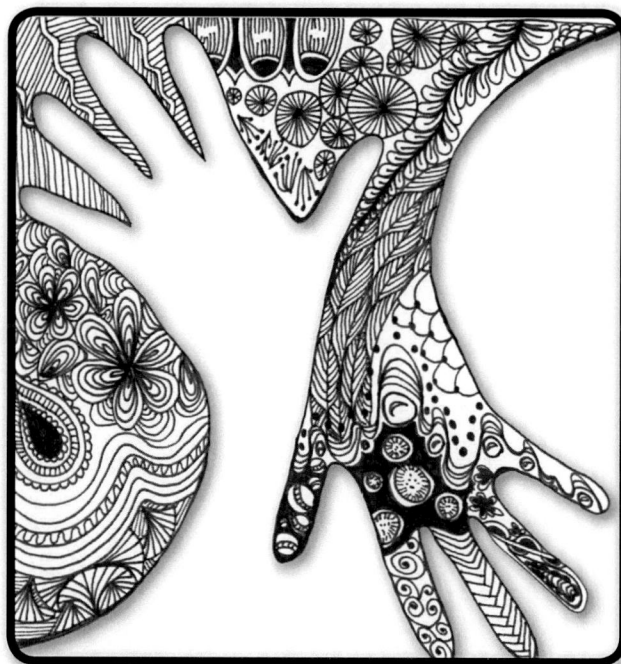

Perform all hand clapping games and activities with partners standing or sitting directly across from each other unless otherwise noted.

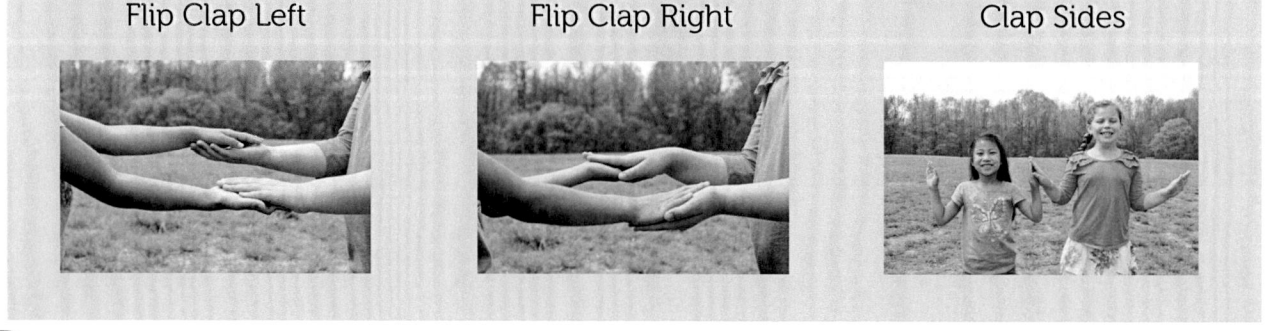

Clap Left	Clap Right	Clap Both

Clap Own	Clap Left High	Clap Right High

Patsch	Clap Right Low	Left Clap Low

Snap	Wrist Flick	Clap Back

Flip Clap Left	Flip Clap Right	Clap Sides

Cross Clap

Clap High

Clap Low

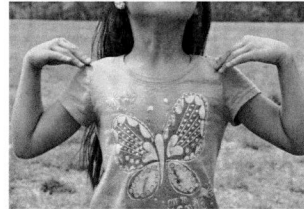

Cross Tap

Tap Shoulders

Backe, Backe, Kuchen

Ba - cke, ba - cke, Ku - chen, der ba - cker hat ge - ru - fen. Wer will gu - ten
Bah-kuh, bah-kuh, Koo - ken, dehr bah-kehr haht geh - roo - fen. Vehr vihl goo-ten

Ku-chen ba-cken, der muss ha-ben sie-ben sa-chen. Zu-cker und Salz, Ei-er und Schmalz,
Koo-ken bah-kehn, dehr moos hah-behn zee-behn zah-kehn. Zoo-kehr oont Sahlts, Eye-ehr oont Shmahlts,

Milch und Mehl, und Sa-fran macht den Ku-chen gelb. Schieb in den O-fen rein.
Mihlk oont Mayl, oont Sah-frahn makt dehn Koo - ken gehlb. Sheeb ihn dehn Oh-fehn rye/n.

Clapping Game - Partners stand in groups of six.
Partners A1/A2 clap high, then middle, then low.
Partners B1/B2 clap middle, then low, then high.
Partners C1/C2 clap low, then high, then middle.

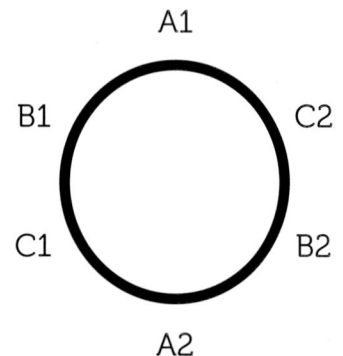

A1
B1   C2
C1   B2
A2

Translation
Bake, bake, bake a cake.
The baker called out!
If you want to bake a good cake,
You need seven ingredients.

Sugar and salt,
Eggs and lard,
Milk and flour,
And saffron makes the cake yellow.
Slide it into the oven.

Clapping Game © 2015 Aimee Curtis Pfitzner. All rights reserved.

BATE, BATE, CHOCOLATE

Ba-te, ba-te, cho-co-la-te, con ar-roz y con to-ma-te. U-no, dos, tres, CHO!

| Cross Tap | Clap Both | Clap R | Clap L | Clap Own | Patsch | Pound Fist | Make Motion |

U-no, dos, tres, CO! U-no, dos, tres, LA! Cho-co-la-te, cho-co-la-te, cho-co-la-te, cho-co-la-te!

| Cross Tap | Clap Both | Clap R | Clap L | Clap Own | Patsch | Pound Fist | Make Motion |

Pound Fist - Pound one fist in open palm.

Make Motion - Make a dramatic, crazy, silly, go big or go home motion.

Translation
Blend the chocolate with rice and tomatoes.

Clapping Game © 2015 Aimee Curtis Pfitzner. All rights reserved.

11

Bella Bimba

Italy

A

Ma, co-me bel-li bel-la bim-ba, bel-la bim-ba, bel-la bim-ba. Ma,
Mah, coh-may bah-lee beh-lah beem-bah, beh-lah beem-bah, beh-lah beem-bah. Mah,

LH Cross
Palm Clap R
RH Cross
Palm Clap L

Fine

co-me bel-li bel-la bim-ba, bel-la bim-ba, bel-la ben.
coh-may bah-lee beh-lah beem-bah, beh-lah beem-bah, beh-lah behn.

LH Cross
Palm Clap R
RH Cross
Palm Clap L

B

D.C. al Fine

Guar-da che pas-sa la vil-la-nel-le. A-gile e snel-la, sa ben dan-zar.
Gar-da khay pah-sah lah vee-ya-neh-lah. Ah-geel ay sneh-lah, sahbehndahn-zahr.

Step Out (Raising Held Hands)   Step In (Lowering Held Hands)

Palm Clap L

RH Cross

A Section -Players stand close together in circle. Own left hand remains palm up in front of body throughout.

Palm Clap L - Own left hand, palm up, right hand claps left hand.

RH Cross - Own right hand crosses to left, claps left side neighbor's hand.

Palm Clap R - Reverse Palm Clap L.

LH Cross - Reverse RH Cross.

Translation
How beautiful is the ballerina.
Down through the village she passes by.
Gracefully dancing, spinning around,
How beautiful is the ballerina.

Clapping Game © 2015 Aimee Curtis Pfitzner. All rights reserved.

BIM BAM

SERBIA/USA

Bim bam, bim bam, bid-dy, bid-dy bam, bid-dy bam, bid-dy, bid-dy bam, bim bam.

SNAP
CLAP OWN
PATSCH

Bim bam, bim bam, bid-dy, bid-dy bam, bid-dy bam, bid-dy, bid-dy bam, bim bam.

SNAP
CLAP OWN
PATSCH

Bim bam, bid-dy, bid-dy bam, bid-dy bam, bid-dy, bid-dy bam, bim bam.

SNAP
CLAP OWN
PATSCH

Bim bam, bid-dy, bid-dy bam, bid-dy bam, bid-dy, bid-dy bam, bim bam.

SNAP
CLAP OWN
PATSCH

Contributed by Sarah Blair, http://ldssplash.com/teens/to_do/handgames/hand_games.htm.
Used with permission.

Teacher Tip - First time, clap only on "Bim." Second time, add snap on "Bam." Third time, add patsch on "Biddy."

Extension - Transfer body percussion to unpitched percussion instruments.
  Bim - Drums
  Bam - Metals
  Biddy - Woods

CHA TSUBO

Cha, cha tsu - bo, cha tsu - bo   cha tsu - bo   ni - wa
Cha,   cha tsoo - boh,   cha tsoo - boh   cha tsoo - boh   nee - wah

RH on L Fist
RH Under L Fist
LH on R Fist
LH Under R Fist

fu - ta   ga nai,   so - ko tot - te   fu - ta nis - shi - yo.
foo - tah   gah nai,   soh - koh toe - tay   foo - tah nih - shih - yoh.

RH on L Fist
RH Under L Fist
LH on R Fist
LH Under R Fist

Collected by Nancy Patson from Yui and Yuta Takahashi. Contributed by Marilyn Shepard. Used with permission.

Clapping Game
Beat 1 - Lid hand (open palm face down) taps fist (jar).
Beat 2 - Switch lid hand to underneath position and tap up to fist.
Beat 3 - Switch hands.
Beat 4 - Put new lid hand underneath fist.

Freeze action during rests. You should end up with a lid on your tea jar.

Translation
Tea jar, tea jar.
The lid is gone.
Take the bottom
and put it on the top.

CUDDLY KOALA

Cud-dly ko-a-la,   cud-dly ko-a-la,   pos-sum too,   pos-sum too.

LAP BOTH
CLAP R
CLAP L
CLAP OWN
PATSCH
STOMP

Two-Hand Turn

Wal-la-bies and wom-bats,   wal-la-bies and wom-bats,   kan-ga-roo,   kan-ga-roo.

LAP BOTH
CLAP R
CLAP L
LAP OWN
PATSCH
STOMP

Jump   Jump

Kangaroo Hop   Kangaroo Hop

Contributed by Susan Curbishley.

Clapping Game and Dance

Partners stand in concentric circles.

Two-Hand Turn - Holding hands, partners turn in complete circle.

Teacher Tip - Teach as an elimination game. First time sing all words; next, "sing inside the head" the words "cuddly koala" while keeping movement; next, omit "possum too", etc., until whole song is internalized.

Danse Tyrolienne

Cross Clap Both / Clap L / Clap R / Clap Own / Patsch

Lyrics (first system):
Tiens voi-la main droite, tiens voi-la main gauche,
Tee/eh vwa-lah meh dwah, *tee/eh vwa-lah meh gohsh,*

Lyrics (second system):
tiens voi-la main droite, main gauche, tiens voi-la les deux.
tee/eh vwa-lah meh dwah, meh gohsh, *tee/eh vwa-la lay duh.*

Contributed by Kay McMeekin.

Cross Clap - Cross hands and clap partner's hands.
Start slowly; increase tempo slightly with each repetition.

Translation
Here you are, right hand,
Here you are, left hand,
Here you are, right hand, left hand,
Here you are, both.

DOUBLE, DOUBLE

ENGLAND

Dou – ble, dou – ble, this, this, dou – ble, dou – ble, that, that.

CLAP BACKS
CLAP BOTH
CLAP OWN

Dou – ble this, dou – ble that, dou – ble, dou – ble, this, that.

CLAP BACKS
CLAP BOTH
CLAP OWN

MARIPOSA

MEXICO

Ma – ri, ma – ri, po, po, ma – ri, ma – ri, sa, sa,

CLAP BACKS
CLAP BOTH
CLAP OWN

ma – ri, po, ma – ri, sa, ma – ri – po – sa.

CLAP BACKS
CLAP BOTH
CLAP OWN

Translation
Mariposa - Butterfly

17

ECI PECI PEC

CROATIA

Lyrics (line 1): E - ci pe - ci pec, ti si ma - li zec. A ja ma - la
Pronunciation (line 1): Eh - tsee pet - see pets, tee see mah - lee zehk. Uh yuh mah - lah

Lyrics (line 2): vje - ver - i - ca, e - ci pe - ci pec.
Pronunciation (line 2): vyeh - veh - ree - kuh, eh - tsee pet - see pets.

Contributed by Ksenija Buric, from **Eci Peci Pec** (Collection of Croatian Songs and Rhymes, by Ksenija Buric). Used with permission.

Flip Clap R - Right hand down and left hand up
Flip Clap L - Left hand down and right hand up

The music begins in triple meter, switches to duple, and ends again in triple.

Translation
Eci peci pec,
You are a little rabbit.
And I'm a little squirrel,
Eci peci pec.

Clapping Game © 2015 Aimee Curtis Pfitzner. All rights reserved.

18

EN LA CALLE VEINTICUATRO (ON 24TH STREET)

SPAIN

En la cal - le vein - ti - cua - tro. En la ca - lle - lle, ___ vein - ti -

FLIP CLAP
CLAP BOTH
CLAP OWN
WRIST FLICK

cua - tro - tro, ___ ha ha - bi - do - do, ___ un as - es - i - na - to - to, ___ u - na vie - ja - ja,

FLIP CLAP
CLAP BOTH
CLAP OWN
WRIST FLICK

___ ma - to un ga - to - to, ___ con la pun - ta - ta, ___ del za - pa - to - to. ___

FLIP CLAP
CLAP BOTH
CLAP OWN
WRIST FLICK

Po - bre vie - ja, po - bre ga - to, po - bre pun - ta, del za - pa - to.

FLIP CLAP
CLAP BOTH
CLAP OWN
WRIST FLICK

Contributed by Teresa Schmitt.

Translation

On Twenty-fourth - orth - orth
Street - eet - eet
There has been - en - en
A murder - der - der
An old lady - dee
Killed a cat - at - at
With the top - op - op
Of the shoe - oo - oo
Poor old lady
Poor cat
Poor top
Of the shoe.

19

Ene Mene Miste

E - ne me - ne Mis - te, Es rap - pelt in der Kis - te.
Eye - neh my - neh Mih - steh, Ehs rah - pelt in dehr Kiss - teh.

E - ne me - ne Meck, und Du bist weg.
Eye - neh my - neh Meck, oont Doo bihst veck.

Collected by Nancy Patson. Contributed by Marilyn Shepard. Used with permission.

Clapping Game - Stand in circle, left hand palm up, right hand palm up in neighbor's left hand.

* One person at a time moves right hand to clap left side neighbor's hand (resting on own left hand).
* Person clapped moves own right hand to clap left side neighbor's hand to left; beat continues around circle.
* Players try to pull hand away on final beat. If player does not pull hand in time but is clapped, player moves to center and begins to create another circle with other eliminated players. Players in center can return to outside circle if they pull hand away on final beat.

Teacher Tip - Tell players to pay attention to their right hand and not worry about their left hand (one hand will be under and other on top).

Translation
Eeny meeny miney mo,
It rattles in the box.
Eeny meeny miney mo,
And out you go.

Klatschen

Clapping

Four White Horses

Carribbean

Four white hor-ses on the riv-er, hey, hey, hey,— up to-mor-row,

Clap High
Clap Own
Clap Sides
Clap Low

up to-mor-row is a rain-y day. Come on and join our sha-dow play. Sha-dow play is a

Clap High
Clap Own
Clap Sides
Clap Low

ripe ba-na-na, hey, hey, hey,— up to-mor-row, up to-mor-row is a rain-y day.

Clap High
Clap Own
Clap Sides
Clap Low

Clapping Game - Partners stand in groups of four.

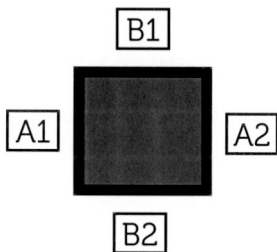

Clap High - A1/A2 clap high while B1/B2 clap low; next pattern A1/A2 clap low while B1/B2 clap high; continue switching between high and low each time.

21

GARGARITA, RITA

ROMANIA

Gar - ga - ri - ta, ri - ta,   zbo - ara in   poien - i - ta,
Gahr - gah-reets - ah, reets - ah,   *zbwa - ra een   poh/een-eets - ah,*

CROSS CLAP BOTH
CLAP BOTH
CLAP OWN
PATSCH

un - de vei   zbu-ra,   a - co - lo va fi ca-sa me - a.
oon - deh vay   zboo-rah,   *ah - koh-loh vah fee cah-sah may - ah.*

CROSS CLAP BOTH
CLAP BOTH
CLAP OWN
PATSCH

Collected by Aimee Pfitzner in Cimpina, Romania.

Giggling and smiling, a little boy in the village of Cimpina taught me this song while telling me the meaning of the Romanian folk legend. When a ladybug lands on a person, you must watch where it flies off to; your future spouse will come from where it lands. I hope he found his "ladybug."

Translation
Ladybug, ladybug,
Fly away into the glade.
Where you will fly,
There will be my home.

Clapping Game © 2015 Aimee Curtis Pfitzner. All rights reserved.

Global Greetings

A. C. Pfitzner
USA

[A]

WAVE
CLAP BOTH
CLAP OWN
PATSCH

How-dy, hi, how are you? Ways to say, Hel-lo! Hel-lo! Hey, what's up, what's hap-pen-ing, and don't for-get yo!

[B]

WAVE
CLAP BOTH
CLAP OWN
PATSCH

Ciao, Ni hao, Jam-bo, Na-ma-ste. Ko-ni-chi-wa, A-lo-ha, Bu-na Zi-ua, G' day!
Chow, Nee how, Jahm-bo, Nah-mah-stay. Ko-nee-chee-wah, Ah-low-ha, Boo-nah Zee-wah, Guh day!

Shake Right   Shake Left   Do Si Do for 6 Beats   Side Step R

© 2015 Aimee Curtis Pfitzner. All rights reserved including public performance for profit.

Dance - Partners face each other in concentric circles.

A Section

Wave - Both hands up in air to wave, "hello." "Yo" - Both pointer fingers point to sky.

B Section

Shake Right - Shake right hand with partner twice.
Shake Left - Shake left hand with partner twice.
Side Step R - Outside circle takes one step to the right to meet new partner.

Ciao - Italian, *Ni hao* - Chinese, *Jambo* - Swahili, *Namaste* - Indian, *Konichiwa* - Japanese, *Aloha* - Hawaiian Islands, *Buna Ziua* - Romanian, *G'day* - Australian

Clapping Game © 2015 Aimee Curtis Pfitzner. All rights reserved.

Hi Lo Chickalo

Scotland

Contributed by Linda Geoghegan, from **Singing Games and Rhymes for Middle Years** (published by National Youth Choir of Scotland). Used with permission.

Clapping Game - Partners face each other in single circle. Left hands remain back to back with partner throughout song.

  Clap R High - Clap right hand above left hand.
  Clap Own L - Clap own left hand held against partner's left hand.
  Clap R Low - Clap right hand below left hand.
  Turn - Turn right to face new partner.

Replay game with right hand back to back with new partner; left hand will clap high, own, and low.

Deceptively simple, the faster you sing, the trickier it gets.

For a challenge, sing the song in its "upside down" version, "Lo, hi, chickahi, chickahi, chickahi. Lo, hi, chickahi, chickahi, lo."

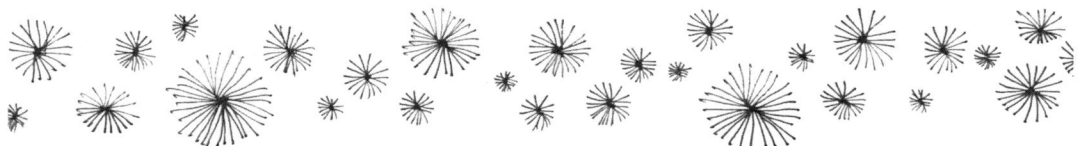

Hokey Pokey Penny a Lump

Scotland

Ho-key po-key pen-ny a lump, the mair ye eat, the mair ye jump. The
(mare) (mare)

mair ye jump, yer sure tae fa. Ho - key po - key that is aa.
(mare) (faw) (ah)

Contributed by Lucinda Geoghegan.

*Fa= fall, aa= all

When I first came across this lovely Scottish chant, I wasn't sure what "fa" meant; I thought (oh, dear) of passing gas! When I contacted Ms. Geoghegan and asked her to clarify, we shared a few giggles via email.

Clapping Game - Partners face each other in single circle.
Jump Turn - Jump to face opposite direction and new partner. Second jump players jump turn to face original partner.

Extension - Partners face each other in concentric circles. Jump to right each time instead of around.

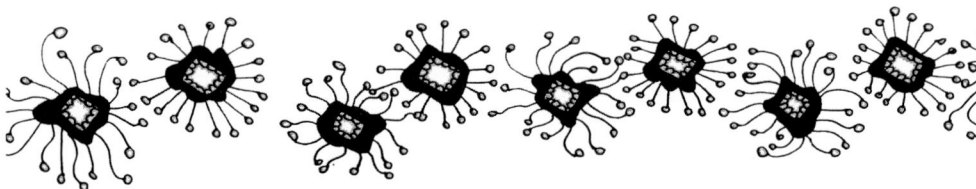

Humpty Dumpty

USA

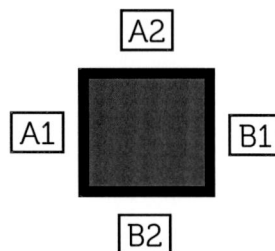

A

Hump-ty Dump-ty, Hump, Hump-ty Dump-ty, Dump-ty, Hump-ty Dump-ty, Hump,

Clap High
Clap Low
Clap Corner
Clap Partner
Clap Own
Patsch

B

Hump-ty Dump-ty, Dump-ty. Twink-le, twink-le lit-tle star, how I won-der what you are,

Clap High
Clap Low
Clap Corner
Clap Partner
Clap Own
Patsch

up a - bove the world so high. Huh! Make it fun - ky now!

Clap High
Clap Low
Clap Corner
Clap Partner
Clap Own
Patsch

Jump Clap

Partners face each other in groups of four.

Clap Partner - A1/A2 - B1/B2
Clap Corner - A1/B2 - B1/A2
Jump Clap - Jump up and clap own hands.
Clap Low: A1/B1 clap low while A2/B2 clap high.
Clap High: A1/B1 clap high while A2/B2 clap low.

A2

A1   B1

B2

Extension - Substitute your favorite nursery rhyme as a new
text in the B Section. Be sure to "Make it funky now!" (A B C D E F G, H I J K L M N O
P, Q R S, T U V. Huh, make it funky now!)

Clapping Game © 2015 Aimee Curtis Pfitzner. All rights reserved.

I Let Her Go Go

Trinidad/Tobago

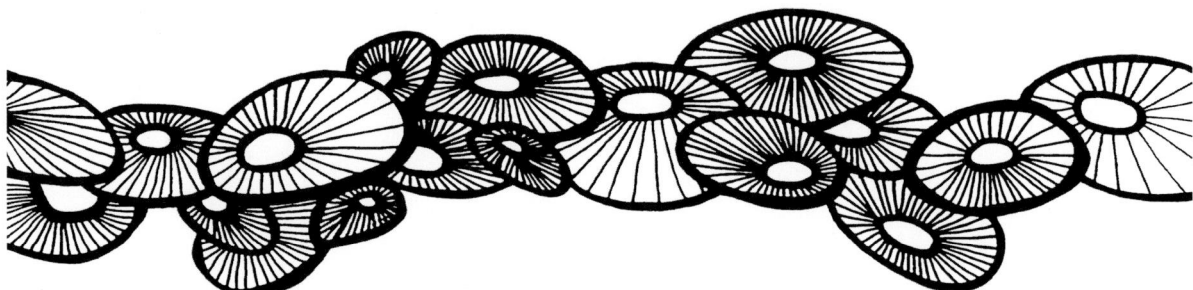

I let her go go, e - ay, I let her
Clap Both
Jump Turn
go go, e - ay, I let her go. I let her go, go, go.
Clap Both
Version 1 Only
Pass Turn
Pass on Version 2 Only
Jump Turn
Version 1 Only

Song, Game and Dance - Partners face each other in single circle.

Version 1

Clap Both - On half note "go," clap and leave hands together while turning to face opposite directions (switch places).

Jump Turn - Jump and turn around to face opposite direction and new partner.

Version 2

Pass Turn - On half note "go," partners pass by right shoulders and wave "bye bye"; meet new partner to clap next "go, go, go."

LADUSHKI

La - dush - ki, la - dush - ki, gdye bwee-lee? U Ba - bush - ki.
Lah - doosh-key, lah-doosh-key, guh/dyeh bweh-lee? Oo Bah-boosh-key.

CLAP L
CLAP R
CLAP BOTH
CLAP OWN

Shtoh yel - lee? Kash - ku. Shtoh pil - lee? Brazh - ku.
Shtoe yeh - lee? Kahsh - koo. Shtoe pill - ee? Brahz - koo.

CLAP L
CLAP R
CLAP BOTH
CLAP OWN

La - dushk - ki, la - dush - ki. Kak bwee-lee u Ba - bush - ki.
Lah - doosh - key, lah - doosh - key. Kahk bwee-lee oo Bah-boosh-key.

CLAP L
CLAP R
CLAP BOTH
CLAP OWN

Contributed by Marilyn Shepard and Natalia Kudimova.

Translation
Ladushki, ladushki. Where have you been? At Grandma's.
Ladushki, ladushki. Where have you been? At Grandma's.
What did you eat? Porridge.
What did you drink? Kifer (a thin yogurt-like drink).
Ladushki, ladushki.
That's how we did at Grandma's house.

My Aunty Anna

My Aun - ty An - na   plays   the   pi - an - a

twen - ty - four   hours   a   day.   Splits!

Collected and contributed by Susan Curbishley. (I wish I could include the sound file of Susan's 5- and 6-year-olds speaking this with their lovely Australian accents. Charming!)

Clapping Game

Jump - Jump up and land with legs slightly apart; repeat chant with legs remaining slightly apart. On next jump, land with legs further apart. Continue until one partner falls and remaining partner wins. Both convulse in helpless laughter. A favorite!!

Mama Celina

Kenya

Ma - ma, ma - ma Ce - li - nah, Ce - li - nah mcho - ko - zi. A -
Mah - mah, mah-mah Seh - lee - nah, Seh - lee - nah mmcho-koh - zee. Ah -

Clap Own
Clap Both
Flip Clap

li - ni - tu - si ma - tu - si ma - ba - ya. Ni - ka - en - da hu -
lee-nee-too-see mah - too-see mah-buy - yah. Nee - kah-ehn - dah hoo -

Clap Own
Clap Both
Flip Clap

- ko town. Ni - kam - pa - ta msi - cha - na mmo - ja. A -
- koh town. Nee - kahm-pah - tah see - cha-nah mo - jah. Ah -

Clap Own
Clap Both
Flip Clap

- ka - niam - bi - a 'a_____ ti - ri - ri'. Si - ku - ju - a hi -
- kah-nee/am-bee - ah ah_____ tee-ray - ray. See - koo-joo - ah ee -

Clap Own
Clap Both
Flip Clap

- o lu - gha. Wa - ma - ma, wa - ma - ma ting - ish - a, ting-ish - a.
- oh loo - gah. Wah - mah - mah, wah-mah-mah tin - gay-sha, tin-gay shay.

Clap Own
Clap Both
Flip Clap

Hands on Hips, Head Bob

Wa - ba - ba, wa - ba - ba ham - jam - bo, ham - jam - bo. Wasi - cha - na, wasi - cha - na war-
Wah-bah-bah, wah-bah-bah ahm-jahm-boh, ahm-jahm-boh. Wahs-kah-nah, wahs-kah-nah wahr-

CLAP OWN
CLAP BOTH
FLIP CLAP

Shake Hands Two Times

em - bo, war - em - bo. Wafu - la - na, wafu - la - na, wach - afu, wach-afu.
ehm-boh, wahr-ehm-boh. Wahf-lah-nah, waf-lah-nah, wash-ahf, wash-ahf.

CLAP OWN
CLAP BOTH
FLIP CLAP

Hands on Hips, Head Bob

Hands at Shoulders,
Flick Fingers Away from Body

Collected and contributed by Tim Gregory, www.KenyaConnects.org.

Clapping Game

Hands on Hips, Head Bob - Put hands on hips and bob head side to side.
Shake Hands Two Times - Shake right hands on "jam."
Hands at Shoulders - Hold hands at shoulder level, fingers closed into loose fists.
Flick Fingers Away from Body - Flick fingers out away from body (flicking dirt away) on "-afu."

Translation

Mama,
Mother Celinah,
Naughty Cellinah.
She scolded me badly.
I went to town.
I met one girl.
She said 'atiriri' (a conjunction word in Kikuyu language).
I did not understand the language.
Mothers, mothers,
Dance, dance.
Fathers, fathers,
Hallo, hallo.
Girls, girls,
Beautiful, beautiful.
Boys, boys,
Dirty, dirty.

The Mexican Woodpecker

Australia

A Mex-i-can wood-peck-er high in a tree went chip chip-pa-chip-pa

chip all the day. He got so am - bi-tious he

wore off his beak. Now you can hear him say...

Oh my beak! Oh my beak! What a sad day

when I lost it. Hear him cry, hear him sigh.

Cross Tap
Clap Both
Clap R/L
Clap Own
Snap
Patsch

What a sor – ry sight to see, poor thing!

Cross Tap
Clap Both
Clap R/L
Clap Own
Snap
Patsch

Contributed by Susan Curbishley.

Teacher Tip
* Teach song first without pattern.
* Teach clapping pattern, "one, two, three, four, five," with the first five motions (through the second Clap Own).
* Add "six, seven, eight" as rests after students perform first five motions.
* Replace rests with next three motions (Cross Tap, Patsch, Snap) as "six, seven, eight."
* Ask half of class to perform clapping pattern while speaking numbers; others perform song.
* Switch parts.

This one is fun yet challenging, perfect for your older kiddos and grown ups. Strain the brain!

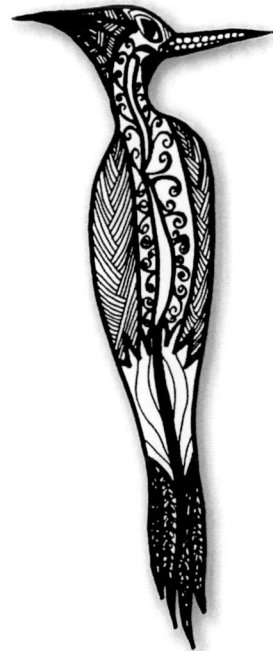

Navajo Happy Song

Navajo

Hi - o   hi - o - ip-pee   a - na,   hi - o   hi - o - ip-pee

1   a __ na,   hi __ o,   hi - o - ip-pee   a - na,   hi __ o,

hi - o - ip-pee   a - na,   hi - o,   hi - o. _____

2   Patsch

3   Patsch LS
      Patsch Own

4   Patsch RS
      Patsch LS
      Patsch Own

5   Floor
      Patsch RS
      Patsch LS
      Patsch Own

34

The following shows the rhythmic score with four staves:

Floor	2/4	
Patsch RS	2/4	
Patsch LS	2/4	
Patsch Own	2/4	

Contributed by Amy Abbott and Christopher Roberts. Collected by Ellen Mc-Cullough-Brabson in the Southwestern United States. Similar version collected by Karen Baldwin in Gallup, New Mexico, and Windowrock, Arizona, in 1977.

Game - Sit in circle, knees close to neighbor's. Song repeats; <u>actions are cumulative.</u>
    1st time - Song only
    2nd time - Patsch
    3rd time - Patsch LS - Patsch leg of left side neighbor twice.
    4th time - Patsch RS - Patsch leg of right side neighbor twice.
    5th time - Floor - Tap floor in front twice.
    6th time - Perform each motion once.

Patsch	Patsch LS	Patsch RS	Tap Floor

35

NAUGHTY CHILD

KENYA

You were sent to the mar-ket, ba-laa m ba-laa, to buy some bread,

ba-laa m ba-laa. But on the way home, ba-laa m ba-laa, you ate the bread,

ba-laa m ba-laa. So back to the mar-ket, ba-laa m ba-laa, but in-

stead you bought a lol-li-pop, ba-laa m ba-laa, you're gon-na be in trou-ble,

ba-laa m ba-laa, 'cause you're a naugh-ty child, yes! ba-laa m ba-laa.

CLAP OWN
CLAP BOTH
FLIP CLAP

36

Collected and contributed by Tim Gregory, www.kenyaconnects.org.

While originally called *Mwanamke Mkorofi* (*Naughty Woman*), the lyrics here have been altered slightly and translated into English to make them more suitable for children, but the message is the same. "Balaa m balaa" means problematic (the "m" is voiced but has no meaning).

NOT LAST NIGHT BUT THE NIGHT BEFORE

AUSTRALIA

Not last night but the night be-fore. Step back, ba-by, step __ back.

Twen-ty-four rob-bers came knock-in' at the door. Step back, ba-by, step __ back. You

should have seen the way those rob-bers ran. Step back, ba-by, step __ back. When

I got out my fry-in' pan. Step back, ba - by, step __ back.

Some flew east and some flew west. Step back, ba-by, step__ back.

| CLAP LEFT |
| CLAP RIGHT |
| CLAP SIDES |
| CLAP BOTH |
| CLAP OWN |

| STEP FORWARD |
| STEP LEFT |
| STEP BACK |

Some flew ov-er the cuc-koo's nest. Step back, ba-by, step__ back.

| CLAP LEFT |
| CLAP RIGHT |
| CLAP SIDES |
| CLAP BOTH |
| CLAP OWN |

| STEP FORWARD |
| STEP LEFT |
| STEP BACK |

Contributed by Susan Curbishley.

Partners face each other in concentric circles.

Step Forward - One step forward with right foot to meet new partner
Step Left - One step to left with left foot
Step Back - One step backward with right foot

Teacher Tip
When practicing "step back, baby, step back," say, "Right, left, right" to simplify Step Back, Step Left, Step Forward.

O Mochi O Tsukimasho

O mo-chi o tsu-ki-ma-sho. O mo-chi o tsu-ki-ma-sho.

Oh moh-chee oh tsoo-kee-mah-shoh. Oh moh-chee oh tsoo-kee-mah-shoh.

Partner 2 — Above / Between / Under / Through / Clap Own

Partner 1 Clap Own

Pet-tan-ko pet-tan-ko, pet-tan pet-tan pet-tan ko. O ko-ne-te o ko-ne-te,

Peh-tahn-koh peh-tahn-koh, peh-tahn peh-tahn peh-tahn-koh. Oh kohn-eh-tay oh kohn-eh-tay,

2 — Above / Between / Under / Through / Clap Own

1 Clap Own

o ko-ne-te, ko-ne-te, ko-ne-te. Ton ton ton ton ton ton ton ton ton ton ton ton ton.

oh kohn-eh-tay, kohn eh tay, kohn-eh-tay. Tawn tawn tawn tawn tawn tawn tawn tawn tawn tawn tawn tawn tawn.

2 — Above / Between / Under / Through / Clap Own

1 Clap Own

Clapping Game

Partner 1 - Clap vertically up and down (think crocodile mouth opening and closing).

Partner 2

    Above - Clap above partner's hands.

    Between - Clap between partner's hands.

    Under - Clap under partner's hands.

    Through - During *"O konete,"* right hand claps own left hand and then right hand moves quickly between partner's "crocodile mouth" left to right (or opposite) in a circular motion. Pretend to brush flour off a countertop.

Above | Between

Under | Through | Clap Own

In traditional stories, a hare, or rabbit, on the face of the moon is making rice cakes (mochi). In this game two people prepare the mochi using a Japanese *usu* (mortar) and *kine* (pestle). Careful timing of the swing of the pestle and the turning of the cooked rice prevents injury; the actions of the game imitate this dangerous baking task.

Translation
The hare is making Sticky Rice on the moon.
Knead, knead, knead, knead-oh.
Pound, pound, pound, pound.
Clap, clap, clap, clap, clap.

Paki Paki

Maori/New Zealand

Clap High
Clap Low
Clap Own

Pa - ki, pa - ki, pa - ki, pa - ki, ta - ma - ri - ki ma.
Pah - kee, pah - kee, pah - kee, pah - kee, tah - mah - ree-kee mah.

Clap High
Clap Low
Clap Own

Pa - ki, pa - ki, pa - ki, pa - ki, ta - ma - ri - ki ma.
Pah - kee, pah - kee, pah - kee, pah - kee, tah - mah - ree-kee mah.

Additional Lyrics

2. Huri, huri, huri, huri, tamariki ma. Huri, huri, huri, huri, tamariki ma.
   (Huri pronounced "who-ree")

3. Rere, rere, rere, rere, tamariki ma. Rere, rere, rere, rere, tamariki ma.
   (Rere pronounced "reh-reh")

4. Hikoi, hikoi, hikoi, hikoi, tamariki ma. Hikoi, hikoi, hikoi, hikoi, tamariki ma.
   (Hikoi pronounced "hee-koy")

5. Oma, oma, oma, oma, tamariki ma. Oma, oma, oma, oma, tamariki ma.
   (Oma pronounced "oh-mah")

6. Peke, peke, peke, peke, tamariki ma. Peke, peke, peke, peke, tamariki ma.
   (Peke pronounced "peh-kay")

7. Whakarongo, whakarongo, tamariki ma. Whakarongo, whakarongo, tamariki ma.
   (Whakarongo pronounced "wah/kah/wrong/oh")

Clapping Game © 2015 Aimee Curtis Pfitzner. All rights reserved.

Contributed by Sharn Daish.

The final "tamariki ma" of every phrase has two possible melodies. Younger children should sing the lower melody. Older students who can sing the octave leap should sing the higher melody. Traditionally, children do the named action (clap, run, jump) while the song is being sung. With older children, consider the following game.

Clapping Game

A1 and A2 are partners and B1 and B2 are partners in groups of four. Partners alternate clapping high and low.

* A1/A2 clap high while B1/B2 clap low.
* A1/A2 clap low while B1/B2 clap high.

For a challenge, try clapping game while performing other motions, turning, walking, running, etc.

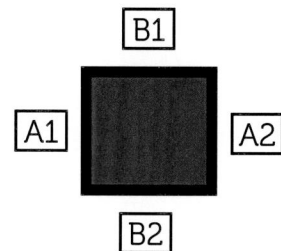

A ukulele provides perfect accompaniment for this song.

The traditional waiata (song) *Paki Paki*, is available on the **Hataitai Playcentre CD and Songbook**, a collection of 20 traditional Maori waiata, available from the Wellington Playcentre website, http://www.wellingtonplaycentre.org.nz/index.php/find-a-centre-mainmenu-39/111-hataitai-playcentres-cd-of-waiata.html.

Translation

Paki - Clap	Rere - Fly	Peke - Jump
Tamariki Ma - Children	Hikoi - Walk	Whakarongo - Listen
Huri - Turn	Oma - Run	

Papegaaitje Leef Je Nog

BELGIUM

Pa - pe - gaai - tje leef je nog?
Pah - pay-gah/ee - tyay layf yay nohkh?

Le - ja dee - ja.
Leh - yuh day - yuh.

Ja me - neer, ik
Yuh meh - nayr, in

ben er nog!
ben air nohkh!

Le - ja dee - ja.
Leh - yuh day - yuh.

'Kheb, m'n e - ten op - ge - ge - ten
Khehb, mn eh - ten ohp - kheh-kheh - ten

en m'n drink - en la - ten staan.
ehn m'n drih/nkh - ehn lah - ten shtahn.

Le - ja dee - ja, poef!
Leh - yuh day - yuh, poof!

CLAP L / CLAP R / CLAP OWN / TAP SHOULDERS / TOUCH HIPS

Tickle

Contributed by Sylvain Dumet and family.

Clapping Game
Tickle - Partners tickle each other on last word.

Pronunciation
G's in Dutch are more like a German "ck"; the back of the tongue is high toward the palate and air moves over it. It helps to think of a cat hissing!

While this song is in Dutch, both Belgian and Dutch are learned and spoken in the country of Belgium.

Translation
Parrot, are you still alive?
Leja deeja.
Yes, sir, I am still alive!
Leja deeja.
I finished my meal already,
but I didn't touch my drinks.
Leja deeja, poef!

Parlez Vous Francais

France/USA

Par - lez vous Fran - cais le ree le ra le re. Par - lez
Pahr - lay voo Frahn - say luh ree luh rah luh ray. Pahr - lay

PASS
HOLD
Roll
R   R   R   R

vous Fran - cais, le ree le ra le re. Par - lez vous Fran - cais le ree le
voo Frahn - say, luh ree luh rah luh ray. Pahr - lay voo Frahn - say luh ree luh

PASS
HOLD
R   R   L   R   L   R   L   L

ra le re. Par - lez vous Fran - cais, le ree le ra le re. Par - lez
rah luh ray. Pahr - lay voo Frahn - say, luh ree luu rah luh ray. Pahr - lay

PASS
HOLD
L   L   L   L   R   L   R   L

Contributed by Sarah Blair, http://ldssplash.com/teens/to_do/handgames/hand_games.htm.
Used with permission.

Translation
Do you speak French?

Cup Game
Seated partners face each other with cup upside down on floor. Grasp cup bottom
with right hand.

Roll - Rattle cup on floor as drum roll while singing this slowly (note fermatas).
Pass - Pass cup right (R) or left (L) as notated. Cup touches floor on notated
beats. During the rest, grab cup being passed by partner.
Hold - While holding cup, tap it left (L) or right (R) in front of you.

Pok Ame Ame

Indonesia

Clap Both / Clap Own / Patsch

Pok a - me a - me be - la - lang ku - pu - ku - pu, te -
Poke ah - may ah - may beh - lah - lahng koo - poo - koo - poo, teh -

puk bi - ar ra - mai pa - gi - pa - gi mi - num su - su.
pook bee - are rah - may pah-gee - pah - gee mee-noom soo - soo.

Contributed by Lin Fadelan.

Translation
Let's clap, clap your hands,
Grasshopper and butterfly.
Clap, clap, and be merry,
And drink your milk in the morning.

Peter Piper Picked a Peck of Pickled Peppers

England
ADAPTED BY A. C. PFITZNER

© 2015 Aimee Curtis Pfitzner. All rights reserved including public performance for profit.

Partners stand in groups of four.

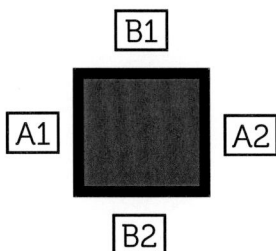

A Section
Clap R Corner - A1/B1 and A2/B2 clap right hands.
Clap L Corner - A1/B2 and A2/B1 clap left hands.

B Section
Clap High - A1/A2 clap high while B1/B2 clap low; next pattern A1/A2 clap low while B1/B2 clap high; continue switching between high and low each time.

Clapping Game © 2015 Aimee Curtis Pfitzner. All rights reserved.

47

Por aquí pasó un caballo

South America

Por a-qui pa-so un ca-ba-llo

con las pa-tas al re-ves.

Version 1

Clap Both
Clap L
Clap R
Clap Own

Version 2

Left High
Left Low
Right High
Right Low
Clap Sides
Clap Both
Clap Own

Si me di-ces cuan-tas tie-ne,

te di-re que die-ci-seis.

Clap Both
Clap L
Clap R
Clap Own

Left High
Left Low
Right High
Right Low
Clap Sides
Clap Both
Clap Own

U-no, dos, tres, cua-tro,

cin-co, seis, sie-te, o-cho,

Clap Both
Clap L
Clap R
Clap Own

Left High
Left Low
Right High
Right Low
Clap Sides
Clap Both
Clap Own

Por aquí pasó un caballo

nue-ve, diez, on-ce, do-ce,   tre-ce, ca-tor-ce, quin-ce, die-ci-seis.

Clap Both	
Clap L	
Clap R	
Clap Own	

Left High	
Left Low	
Right High	
Right Low	
Clap Sides	
Clap Both	
Clap Own	

Contributed by Teresa Schmitt.

Version 1 - Partners
Version 2 - Groups of four

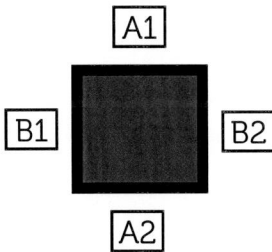

A1

B1   B2

A2

Translation
A horse passed by here
With his legs on backwards.
If you ask me how many he has,
I'll tell you sixteen.
1, 2, 3, 4,
5, 6, 7, 8,
9, 10, 11, 12,
13, 14, 15, 16.

Right High - A1/A2 clap right hands high while B1/B2 clap right hands low.
Left High - A1/A2 clap left hands high while B1/B2 clap left hands low.

Clapping Game © 2015 Aimee Curtis Pfitzner. All rights reserved.

RITSCH RATSCH

SWEDEN

A

Ritsch, ratsch, fi-li-boom, boom, boom, fi-li-boom, boom, boom, fi-li-boom, boom, boom.

CLAP SIDES
CLAP BOTH
CLAP OWN
PATSCH

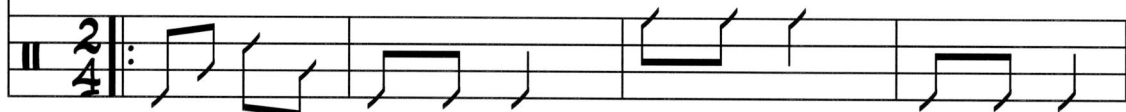

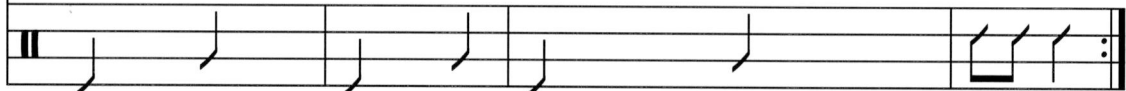

Ritsch, ratsch, fi-li-boom, boom, boom, fi-li-boom, boom, boom, fi-li-boom.

CLAP SIDES
CLAP BOTH
CLAP OWN
PATSCH

B

Swe-dish pan-cakes, Swe-dish pie, lin-gon-ber-ries, lin-gon-ber-ries, ay, yi, yi!

CLAP SIDES
CLAP BOTH
CLAP OWN
PATSCH

Outside Circle Steps Rght to Next Partner

Clapping Game - Partners face each other in concentric circles.

Translation
Nonsense words until "Swedish pancakes, Swedish pie..."

Clapping Game © 2015 Aimee Curtis Pfitzner. All rights reserved.

Ron macaron tinterro

Costa Rica

Ron ma-ca-ron tin - ter-ro, a la ma-guao te-o, te-o, tin tin tin, o
Ron mac-ah-ro teen - tare-oh, ah lah mah-wow tay-oh, tay-oh, teen teen teen, oh

Pass Clap
Clap 3x

te - o, te - o, tin tin tin, u - no, dos, tres.
tay - oh, tay - oh, teen teen teen, oo - no, dohs, trehs.

Pass Clap
Clap 3x

Collected and contributed by Marilyn Shepard.

Elimination Clapping Game - Stand
with hands out to sides, left hand palm up,
right hand palm up in neighbor's left hand.

> ### Translation
> Nonsense words until "uno, dos, tres"; numbers one, two, and three in Spanish.

* One person at a time moves right hand to clap left side neighbor's hand.
* Person clapped moves own right hand to clap left side neighbor's hand.
* Beat continues around circle until one player claps "tin tin tin" three times on neighbor's hand.
* Player about to be clapped on "tres" tries to pull hand away before being clapped. If clapped, player is out.
* Eliminated player goes to center; as more eliminated players join, they begin game in center.

With two circles going, inner circle players clapped on "tres" remain in inner circle; if they pull away successfully, they return to outer circle. Kids get competitive and moans, groans and uproarious laughter ensue.

Teacher Tip
Tell players to pay attention to their right hand and not worry about their left hand (one hand will be under and other on top).

SI, SI, SI!

Si, si, si! No, no, no! Por ar-ri-ba, por a-ba-jo,

por un la-do, por el o-tro, por los dos. In-ten-ta-lo o-tra vez!

Collected and contributed by Marilyn Shepard.

Translation
Yes, yes, yes! No, no no!
Clap up high, clap down low.
To one side and to the other.
Then do both. Try again.

Son Macaron

Unknown

Son mac-a-ron son Fe - ri - on. Ma-ri-on, Ma-ri-on, Le-ah, Le-ah, tap, tap, tap.

Le - ah, Le - ah, tap, tap, tap. One beat, two beat, three beat, catch!

Unknown origins; some sources claim Yugoslavia, others Latin America.

Pronunciation
Macaron, son, Ferion, Marion - All are sung like the word "on."

Translation
Nonsense words until "One beat, two beat..."

Elimination Clapping Game - Stand with hands out to sides, left hand palm up, right hand palm up in neighbor's left hand.

* One person at a time moves right hand to clap left side neighbor's hand.
* Person clapped moves own right hand to clap left side neighbor's hand.
* Beat continues around circle until "catch."
* Player about to be clapped on "catch" tries to pull hand away before being clapped. If clapped, player is out.
* Eliminated player goes to center; as more eliminated players join, they begin game in center.

    With two circles going, inner circle players clapped on "catch" remain in inner circle; if they pull away successfully, they return to outer circle.

Teacher Tip
Tell players to pay attention to their right hand and not worry about their left hand (one hand will be under and other on top).

Extension
Eliminated player moves to a designated space to play an unpitched percussion instrument on chosen word (Marion, for example). As game continues, player plays the rhythm of "Marion, Marion." The next eliminated player could join in playing "Marion" with another instrument or form a new group (at teacher's discretion) to play on "tap, tap, tap" with another unpitched percussion instrument.

Tepuk Tepuk Tangan

Indonesia

Te - puk, te - puk tan - gan, ber - pu - tar - pu - tar,
Teh - pook, teh - pook tahn - gahn, behr - poo - tar - poo - tar,

**Clap Both
Clap Own**

Turn Around in
Place Quickly

tang - gan di ke - pa - la, tan - gan di - ping - gang.
tahn - gahn dee keh - pal - lah, tahn - gahn dee - ping - ahng.

**Clap Both
Clap Own**

Tap Head

Hands on Hips
Move Left, Right

Contributed by Lin Fadelan.

Translation
Clap, clap, your hands.
Turn around again.
Put your hands on your head,
Then hands on your hips.

Clapping Game © 2015 Aimee Curtis Pfitzner. All rights reserved.

XAXB

FRANCE

Al – pha – bay!   X   X   A   A,   X   X   bay   bay.
Ahl – fah – bay!   *X   X   ah   ah,   X   X   bay   bay,*

FISTS
CLAP BACKS
CLAP OWN

X   A   X   bay,   X   al – pha – bay!
X   ah   X   bay,   X   ahl – fah – bay!

FISTS
CLAP BACKS
CLAP OWN

Lyrics have the "bay" spelled out, but the "A" is shown as the single letter instead of the phonetic "ah."

Sto Mi E Milo

Macedonia

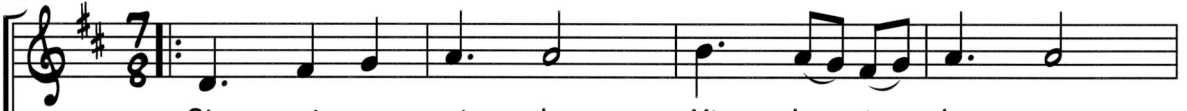

Sto mi e mi - lo. Mi - lo i dra - go.
Sto me eh mee - loh. Mee - loh eh drah - go.

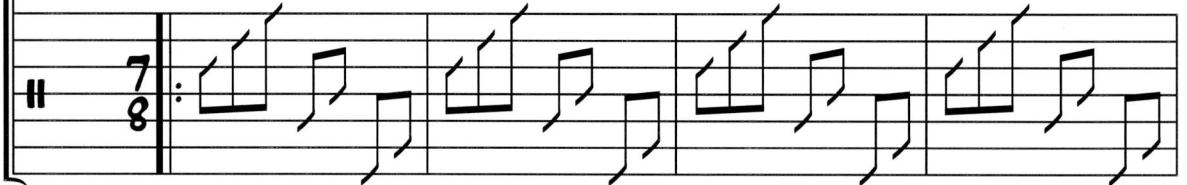

Vo stru - ga gra - da, ma mo du - kjan da i - mam.
Voh stroo - gah grah - dah, mah moh doo - kahn dah ee - mahm.

Le - le va - raj mo - me, mo - me ka - li - no,
Leh - leh va - rye moh - meh, moh - meh kah - lee - noh,

Vo Stru - ga gra - da, ma mo du - kjan da i - mam.
Voh Stroo - gah grah - dah, mah moh doo - kahn dah ee - mahm.

56

Contributed by Lucinda Geoghegan, from **Singing Games and Rhymes for ages 9 to 99** (published by National Youth Choir of Scotland). Used with permission.

Clapping Game by Lucinda Geoghegan - Play without partners.

Macedonian is a Slavic language spoken by people around the world including the countries of the Former Yugoslav Republic of Macedonia (FYROM), and in Albania, Bulgaria, Greece, Serbia, the USA, Australia, Canada, Romania and Serbia.

Translation
How pleased and happy I would be
To have a shop in the town of Struga.
Hey, Kalina.
To have a shop in the town of Struga.

Shoulder L	Shoulder R	Snap L

Snap R	Patsch L	Patsch R

Zoom, Zoom and ABC

Kenya

Zoom zoom but-ee one, two, tha-ree. But-ee to but-ee men-tion. But-ee, but-ee but

Zoom zoom but-ee one, two, tha-ree. But-ee to but-ee men-shun. But-ee, but-ee but

Clap High
Clap Low
Clap Own
Side Clap 1
Side Clap 2

2 Hand Twist

wa - naim - ba.   But-ee, but-ee but   wa - na - ru - ka.   But-ee, but-ee but

wa - na/eem-bah.   But-ee, but-ee but   wah-nah-roo-kah.   But-ee, but-ee but

A,   B,   C,   D,   E,   F,   G,   H,   I,   J,   K,   L,   M,   N,

O,   P,   Q,   R,   S,   T,   U,   V,   W,   X,   Y,   Z!

Collected and contributed by Tim Gregory of www.KenyaConnects.com. Used with permission.

58

Clapping Game - Players stand in groups of four.

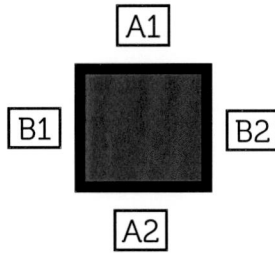

Two-Hand Twist - A1/A2 hold hands and B1/B2 hold hands; right hands pull, left hands push (gently) to create twist.
Clap High - A1/A2 claps high while B1/B2 claps low.
Clap Low - A1/A2 claps low while B1/B2 claps high.
Side Clap 1 - A2/B1 and A1/B2 clap hands.
Side Clap 2 - A2/B2 and A1/B1 clap hands.

Notes from Tim - When learning English, Swahili speakers speak words correctly. When singing songs with English words, they almost always add another syllable onto one-syllable words, hence the "but-ee" for "but" and "tha-ree" for "three."

In Kenya, songs are frequently in English and Swahili.

This game teaches verb conjugation as well as the alphabet. Other verbs could be substituted for the verbs used, *wanaimba* (they are singing) and *wanaruka* (they are jumping).
Wanacheza - They are playing (Wah.nah.chay.zah).
Wanatembea - They are walking (Wah.nah.tehm.bay.ah).
Wanalia - They are crying (Wah.nah.lee.ah).

The game changes constantly as teachers customize it for the words they are teaching.

Translation
Zoom zoom but one two three
But to but mention
But, but, but,
They are singing
But, but, but,
They are jumping
But, but, but
A, B, C...

This Book's Story

My colleagues and I talked about the challenges of teaching in this "digital age" with "digital natives" (students who have grown up using technology) in an end-of-year faculty meeting. One teacher remarked children today don't know what to do with themselves on the bus when they are not allowed to get out their electronic devices; we discussed how kids can't tolerate even the smallest amount of boredom. I remembered how friends and older cousins taught me clapping songs and games on the bus back in Maine. I realized my students needed those same games and songs, and I made a commitment to teach some of these clapping songs the next school year.

When my initial social media post about clapping games got 2,000 hits, I knew others across the world were interested just as I was. But during my research, I could not find a single published collection of songs, games, rhymes, and chants from around the world which also included music notation and directions. I decided to create such a comprehensive volume and reached out through family, friends, parents of students, and strangers asking for songs and games from their childhoods and countries. As the sharing grew, my search for more games and chants became almost obsessive; could I find something from the Maori culture? How about from Nigeria or Croatia? Where was the limit? Was the world truly so small that sending a request written in English, translated online, and sent electronically via email to an email address (also located online) would return a song or rhyme in another language accessible to young children? YES! I was amazed at how kind and giving music teachers and others shared their resources. Ksenija Buric in Croatia sent me her entire collection of Croatian rhymes and songs. An online video led me to Tim Gregory, Director of KenyaConnects.com, and a phone conversation with him (in itself inspiring and uplifting) led me to contacts he had in Indonesia, which led me to yet other contacts. I marvel how incredibly small (thanks to technology), yet how vast our planet is, and I delight in wonderful new friends I will probably never meet in person.

These songs, chants, and rhymes are rich in similarities, yet often slightly different in tunes, words, or rhythms. Notating these examples of the world's rich diversity of oral music shouldn't mean they are carved in stone or drawn in permanent marker. The beauty of oral tradition allows these songs, chants, and rhymes to change depending on regional cultures, time periods, and peoples performing them.

This collection is a simple curved line at the beginning of an artist's sketch. We can now continue to fill in the design.

Aimee Curtis Pfitzner

Acknowledgments

Thank you, **Susan Curbishley,** in Australia; I loved the email conversations and your lovely children with their Aussie accents chanting "My Aunty Anna."

Miriam Schiff from Johannesburg, South Africa, our phone conversation made us friends and one day we WILL meet.

Lucinda Geoghegan in Scotland, I thoroughly enjoyed our email conversations and know when we meet one day, we will have a highly animated conversation on folk song etymology.

Tim Gregory of KenyaConnects.org, thank you for sending your crews around Kenya to record the children. It was amazing to watch and listen to them "almost live." Tim, you are an inspiration to me; your passion for children and music education is contagious to all who meet you, I'm sure.

Aziza Powell of cocojams.com, you are an incredibly interesting historian with a true passion for folk songs and their relationship with popular music; what a collection and legacy.

Teresa Schmitt, my Spanish teacher at school, you were so helpful; gracias, amiga.

Marilyn Shepard, I enjoyed our phone conversations immensely and am so very grateful for all that you shared.

Brent and Karen Holl, editors at Beatin' Path Pub, you're cool dudes; thank you for driving the process and for your encouragement.

Tommi Poland and my daughter, **Caiya,** thank you for being my "hand models" and for your patience in taking the pictures.

Friends and family who "put the word out" and to all of you who so kindly contributed, I cannot thank you enough.

Lastly, and most importantly, thank you to my husband **Cary** for your encouragement and patience with me.

Supplemental resources are available online at http://bppub.net/AimeeCurtisPfitzner. Included are full color visuals in .pdf and .jpg formats suitable for presentation stations or projection and videos of many games.

Purchasers can request login information to gain access to these materials at http://bppub.net/AimeeCurtisPfitzner.

Beatin' Path Publications

Music That Works!

Circle 'Round the Zero (Book) - Maureen Kennedy $29.95
Play Chants and Singing Games of City Children

Forgotten Treasures (Book) - Konnie Saliba $29.95
Folk Songs, Games, and Activities for Orff Classes

In the Modes (Book/CD ROM) - Chris Judah-Lauder $34.95
Instrumental Pieces for Orff Ensemble using the Modes

Simply Speaking (Book/CD ROM) - Sue Mueller $24.95
Speech Activities for Music Classes Grades K - 6

Simply Beginning (Book/CD ROM) - Sue Mueller $29.95
Beginning Activities for Music Classes Grades K - 6

Ensemble (Book/CD) - Brent M. Holl $24.95
Easy and Intermediate Pieces for Orff Ensemble Grades 4 - 8

Wood Songs (Book/CD) - Brent M. Holl $24.95
Ensemble Pieces for Xylophones and Marimbas Grades 4 - 8

Canons Too! (Book) - Brent M. Holl $12.95
An Active Study in Part Singing for Grades 4 - 8

Elementary Guitar (Book) - Dr. Connie Hale $24.95
A Chord Method Featuring Folk Songs

Modal Mosaic (Book/CD ROM) - Robert A. Amchin $34.95
Modal Pieces with Lesson Plans for Orff Classes

All editions are available from
Beatin' Path Publications, LLC
302 East College Street, Bridgewater, VA 22812
beatinpath@mac.com • 540-478-4833
www.beatinpathpublications.com